D1118800

WITHDRAWN

Courageous Heroes of the American West

Zebulon Pike
Courageous Rocky Mountain Explorer

William R. Sanford and Carl R. Green

Enslow Publishers, Inc.
40 Industrial Road
Box 398
Berkeley Heights, NJ 07922
USA

http://www.enslow.com

Original edition published as *Zebulon Pike: Explorer of the Southwest* in 1996.

Library of Congress Cataloging-in-Publication Data

Sanford, William R. (William Reynolds), 1927–

  Zebulon Pike : courageous Rocky Mountain explorer / William R. Sanford and Carl R. Green.

     p. cm. — (Courageous heroes of the American West)

  "Original edition published as Zebulon Pike: Explorer of the Southwest in 1996."

  Includes index.

   Summary: "Examines the life of Zebulon Pike, including his childhood on the frontier, his days
as a soldier, exploring the Rocky Mountains and the Southwest, and his legacy in American
history"—Provided by publisher.

  ISBN 978-0-7660-4012-0

   1. Pike, Zebulon Montgomery, 1779–1813—Juvenile literature. 2. Explorers—West (U.S.)—
Biography—Juvenile literature. 3. West (U.S.)—Biography—Juvenile literature. 4. West (U.S.)—
Discovery and exploration—Juvenile literature. 5. West (U.S.)—History—To 1848—Juvenile
literature. I. Green, Carl R. II. Title.

  F592.P653S26 2013

  978'.02092—dc23

  [B]

                        2011051629

Future editions:

Paperback ISBN 978-1-4644-0095-7

ePUB ISBN 978-1-4645-1002-1

PDF ISBN 978-1-4646-1002-8

Printed in the United States of America

032012 Lake Book Manufacturing, Inc., Melrose Park, IL

10 9 8 7 6 5 4 3 2 1

To Our Readers: We have done our best to make sure all Internet addresses in this book were active
and appropriate when we went to press. However, the author and the Publisher have no control over,
and assume no liability for, the material available on those Internet sites or on other Web sites they
may link to. Any comments or suggestions can be sent by e-mail to comments@enslow.com or to the
address on the back cover.

☘ Enslow Publishers, Inc., is committed to printing our books on recycled paper. The paper in every
book contains 10% to 30% post-consumer waste (PCW). The cover board on the outside of each book
contains 100% PCW. Our goal is to do our part to help young people and the environment too!

Illustration Credits: AP Images / Stephanie S. Cordle, p. 25; © 2011 Clipart.com, a division of Getty
Images, pp. 11, 15, 16; Enslow Publishers, Inc., p. 23; © Enslow Publishers, Inc. / Paul Daly, p. 1;
The Granger Collection, NYC, pp. 6–7, 38, 42; John Hoffman / Photos.com, a division of Getty
Images, p. 44; Library of Congress Prints and Photographs, pp. 33, 36; National Archives and Records
Administration, p. 29; ullstein bild / The Granger Collection, NYC, p. 20.

Cover Illustration: © Enslow Publishers, Inc. / Paul Daly.

Contents

Authors' Note

Soaring more than fourteen thousand feet, Pikes Peak dominates the southern end of the Rocky Mountains. The mountain takes its name from the man who first explored this region for the United States. His name was Zebulon Montgomery Pike. Fifty-two years after Pike first sighted the towering peak, a gold rush took place seventy-five miles away at Cherry Creek. Prospectors hurried across the plains with "Pikes Peak or Bust" painted on their wagons. Few of them knew the full story of the trailblazer who opened the way for them. Zebulon Pike's adventurous 1806–1807 journey gave Americans their first glimpse of the southwestern segment of the Louisiana Purchase. This book tells the true story of his life.

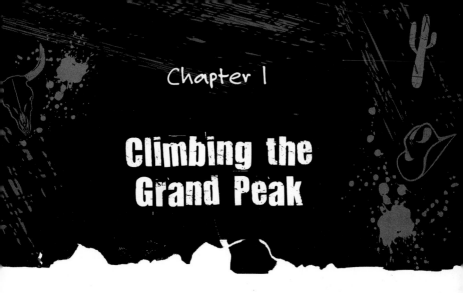

Chapter 1

Climbing the Grand Peak

The date was November 15, 1806. The journey was not going well, but Lieutenant Zebulon Pike pushed on. He had led his small party west from St. Louis five months before. Out on the Great Plains, the weather had turned cold. Their horses found only bark and cottonwood leaves to feed on. One by one, the animals had fallen and died.

That afternoon, a mountain range appeared on the horizon. Zeb pulled out his spyglass. The tallest peak, he wrote later, "appeared like a small blue cloud."

Zeb's men briefly forgot their months of hardship. They whooped and cheered joyously at the sight of "the Mexican mountains." The explorer marked the range in his notebook. Today, we know he was looking at the Front Range of the Rocky Mountains. Zeb guessed that he had found a natural boundary between the Louisiana Territory and New Mexico.

This 1822 engraving shows the broken table lands seen by Zebulon Pike on his expedition west in 1806 as his party approached the Front Range of the Rocky Mountains. After months of hardship crossing the barren plains in winter, Zeb's small party celebrated the sight of "the Mexican mountains."

In the clear air, the highest peak looked quite close. Zeb turned northwest toward what he called the Grand Peak. Twenty-five miles and two days later, however, the mountain looked no closer. A chance meeting with a Pawnee war party added new dangers. Only a quick retreat saved the outnumbered white men from a bloody fight.

On November 24, the men built a small fort next to the Arkansas River. The city of Pueblo, Colorado, now stands on the site. At noon, Zeb led three men toward the Grand Peak. Because the mountain looked

so close, the small group traveled light. At sunset, they were still trudging across the prairie. That night, they made a dry camp under a cedar tree.

The next day, the men crossed twenty-two miles of wooded hills. Night found them camped below what looked like the Grand Peak. They drank from a spring and killed two buffalo for supper. Zeb took measurements and added new details to his map.

Looking up, Zeb made a bad guess. He told his men that they could make the climb and return in a day. To lighten their packs, they left blankets and food behind. Steep, slippery rocks soon turned the "easy" climb into a nightmare. Darkness found the climbers well below the summit. They shivered through a long night in a snow cave.

The next day's climb took the climbers through deep snow. Far below, clouds moved across the prairie. Zeb said the clouds looked like "the ocean in a storm," with wave piled on wave. An hour later, the men reached the top of the peak. Zeb saw at once that this was not Grand Peak. The massive mountain lay waiting, fifteen miles farther on. It towered twice as high above the plain as Cheyenne Mountain, the peak he was standing on. "No human being," Zeb thought, "could have ascended to its pinical [sic]."

The hungry men took a faster route back to their base camp. There they found that ravens had scattered their food cache. Thanksgiving dinner was a piece of deer's rib and a partridge. After some buffalo passed within rifle range the next day, the party ate better. The weary men reached their fort on November 29.

Zeb Pike never did climb the mountain that bears his name. He was not even the first to see Pikes Peak. American Indians and Spanish traders had known about it for two centuries or more. It was Dr. Edwin James who conquered the peak. That was in 1820, just fourteen years after Zeb said it could not be done. By then, mapmakers were using Zeb's name on their charts. Deserved or not, the name stuck.

A road to the top of Pikes Peak opened in 1915. Zeb would have been amazed.

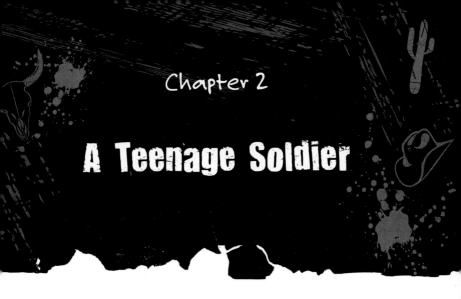

Chapter 2

A Teenage Soldier

In 1775, Americans rose in revolt against Great Britain. As armies clashed, wives kept the home fires burning. One of these resourceful women was Isabella Pike of Lamberton, New Jersey. On January 5, 1779, Isabella gave birth to a son. She named him for his soldier father, Zebulon. Later, the couple gave the boy a middle name, Montgomery. His name paid tribute to a hero of the American Revolution.

Peace returned to the new nation in 1783. Pike left the army and moved his family to eastern Pennsylvania. Bad luck seemed to follow them there. The rocky soil produced poor harvests. Two of the Pikes' three boys fell ill with tuberculosis. Only little Zeb and his sister Maria escaped the dreaded disease.

Schooling was hard to come by. Zeb went to country schools from time to time. His parents also taught him at home. Mathematics was one of his strengths. Later, as an adult, he taught himself more math and science. The nearby woods taught other useful lessons. Zeb became a crack shot and a skilled woodsman.

The lure of cheap land drew farmers west. As the frontier advanced, the Shawnee, Delaware, and other Old Northwest Tribes took to the warpath. The call for soldiers led Zeb's father to join the state militia. Late in 1791, Captain Pike was serving near what is now Greenville, Ohio. Faced with their first enemy fire, many soldiers broke and ran. Pike staged a fighting retreat that saved a number of lives.

Congress sent the regular army to replace the militia. General "Mad Anthony" Wayne soon whipped his command into shape. In April 1793, Wayne put Captain Pike in charge of Fort Washington. Pike moved his family to the site on the Ohio River. There, fourteen-year-old Zeb met General James Wilkinson. The meeting helped shape Zeb's future.

Wilkinson was a poor role model. Scandals had twice forced him to resign from the army. He was in uniform only because the nation needed well-trained officers. When Zeb first met him, Spanish officials were paying the general to help bring Kentucky under

Fifteen-year-old private Zebulon Pike claimed he saw his first military action as part of his father's army unit at the Battle of Fallen Timbers. In the battle, General "Mad Anthony" Wayne led the American troops to victory over the Northwest Tribes.

their control. Wilkinson also kept the Spanish supplied with American secrets. Most of those "secret plans" were fakes that he created himself.

Zeb had always wanted to be a soldier. In 1794, the fifteen-year-old joined his father's unit. Before long, Private Pike was marching off to battle. The Northwest Tribes again were fighting to keep settlers off their land. In August, General Wayne crushed the tribes at the Battle of Fallen Timbers. Zeb later claimed that he saw his first action there.

Young Zeb soon rose to the rank of sergeant. The army put him to work as a quartermaster. His job was to make sure that supplies reached the frontier forts. The food and gunpowder came down the Ohio River by barge and keelboat. One of Zeb's stops along the river was his father's command, now at Fort Massac.

General Wayne died in 1796. Friends in Washington helped Wilkinson step into Wayne's shoes. The new commander kept his eye on Zeb Pike. In 1799, he commissioned his young friend as a second lieutenant. Eight months later, Zeb rose to first lieutenant. He yearned for adventure, but his duties kept him close to the river. For five years, Zeb shipped supplies to a chain of downstream forts.

In 1801, Zeb fell in love with his cousin. Clarissa (Clara) Brown was the daughter of Zeb's wealthy uncle, Captain James Brown. Although it was not uncommon for cousins to marry at that time, Brown still did not want Clara to wed a lowly lieutenant. That did not stop the young lovers. Zeb and Clara ran off and married without his blessing.

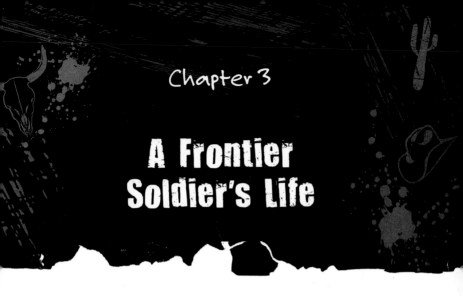

Chapter 3

A Frontier Soldier's Life

Zeb and Clara started married life at a frontier outpost called Fort Knox. The fort stood beside the Wabash River in what was then known as the Indiana Territory. It was a grim, lonely place. A traveler described it as " . . . a mean looking village on the flat prairie near the river. The low banks were covered with weeds rotten from the floods. The village water was filthy. The air stank."

When the weather was good, Zeb and Clara rode and hunted. In the evening, they played cards or went to dances. Spring was a time for tending a small garden. Zeb drew strength from Clara's love. The couple needed that strength. Four of their children died young. Only one daughter survived.

At age twenty-one, Zeb stood five feet eight inches tall. A friend noted that he was "square and robust.

His complexion was ruddy, eyes blue, light hair and good features." The friend also described Zeb as a gentleman and a good soldier. In an age when many drank to excess, Zeb drank very little. He preferred to read. In his free time, he studied military tactics and French. He also picked up a little Spanish.

Zeb filled his letters with good advice. To his sister Maria, he wrote: "You should employ what leisure time you can command in reading and writing. Your words are generally pretty well spelt [sic], but the writing is bad. Practice more and learn to write without quite so much flourish." He also scolded his ten-year-old brother. "Unless you make rapid advances in learning, . . . you are lost," he wrote to George.

The fort's soldiers amused themselves by drinking, gambling, and fighting. Zeb scorned such vices. He punished slackers and drunks with whippings. Despite this, his men held him in high regard. Unlike some officers, he shared their dangers and hardships.

In 1803, the army put Zeb in charge of Fort Kaskaskia in Illinois. The fort stood beside the Mississippi River. St. Louis lay fifty miles south. Some eighty families crowded into a hodgepodge of crude houses. It was not a healthy place. Zeb almost died from a case of measles. Clara and the children

At age twenty-one, Zeb's friends described him as a gentleman and a good soldier. Zeb preferred to read, write, and study military tactics rather than join his fellow soldiers when they wasted their time drinking and gambling.

suffered from fevers. It was Wilkinson who broke the dull routine. From time to time, the general sent Zeb to Washington, D.C., with his dispatches.

Lieutenant Meriwether Lewis stopped at the fort. He was recruiting men for a great journey. The United States had split the huge Louisiana Territory into two parts. The Orleans Territory lay to the south. Lewis and Captain William Clark were setting out to explore the Upper Louisiana Territory. President Jefferson hoped they could find a route to the Pacific Ocean. Zeb wanted to join them, but his duties tied him down.

Wilkinson, now governor of Upper Louisiana, played more sly games. He told the Spanish that Lewis and Clark would pass through their lands. The false

General James Wilkinson gave Zebulon Pike his first opportunity to lead an exploration of uncharted territory.

report helped convince them that Wilkinson was worth his pay. Within his own government, Wilkinson had a friend in Vice President Aaron Burr. It was Burr who had helped make him governor. A year later, in 1804, Burr killed Alexander Hamilton in a duel. Hamilton's death ended Burr's hopes of someday running for president. Undaunted, he set out to enlist Wilkinson in a plot to invade Mexico.

Wilkinson pressed on with plans to learn more about the territory he governed. In August 1805, he sent Lieutenant George Peter westward along the Osage River. Only then did Wilkinson tell his superiors what he had done. Peter's task, he wrote, was to find sites for forts. He also would collect data on water and timber. The general did not mention his own scheme. Peter's report, he hoped, would help him expand his fur-trading interests.

Wilkinson sent a second set of orders to Zeb Pike. Zeb left Fort Kaskaskia and reported to St. Louis. The adventurous young man's luck had changed. It was his turn to go exploring.

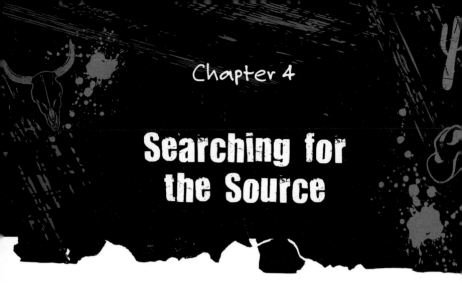

Chapter 4

Searching for the Source

Zeb was twenty-six and burned with ambition. Like Lewis and Clark, he was eager to explore new lands. First, he moved his family to Fort Belle Fontaine near St. Louis. Then he turned to the task Wilkinson had given him.

Where Lieutenant Peter had gone west, Zeb was headed north. Wilkinson pointed him toward Leech Lake in present-day Minnesota. The lake was thought to be the source of the Mississippi River. On the way, Zeb was to take notes on resources, landforms, and weather. He also was told to observe the local American Indians. If the chance came, he was to bargain for the right to build forts and trading posts. If Zeb met British traders, he was to remind them that they were on American land. They could stay, but they must pay U.S. customs duties. Most of all, they must not stir up trouble among the tribes.

Zeb spent two thousand dollars on a seventy-foot keelboat and its cargo. Army agents supplied flour, pork, whiskey, gunpowder, salt, and tobacco. Zeb added gifts of dogs and tents for the American Indians. His kit of scientific tools contained only three items. He made do with a watch, a thermometer, and a device to measure latitude.

Zeb led twenty men upriver on August 9. The trip went smoothly at first. Favoring winds helped the keelboat make up to forty miles a day. When the wind failed, the men pushed the boat upstream with long poles. At times, they had to trudge along the bank, towing the boat with ropes. For energy, each man ate seven or eight pounds of meat a day. The cook often boiled the meat with flour and wild rice to make a stew. The men's big appetites kept two hunters busy.

Zeb and his men met traders, miners, and trappers along the way. American Indians appeared, eager to trade for cloth, knives, and whiskey. In late September, Zeb reached the site of present-day Minneapolis. He thought it looked like a good place for a fort. On September 23, he held a council with the Sioux. The local chiefs sold him a hundred thousand acres of land

Zebulon Pike steers his keelboat across Lake Pepin as his expedition travels up the Mississippi. Waiting on shore to welcome the explorer and his men are a group of American Indians. The local Sioux chiefs agreed to sell the explorer a hundred thousand acres of land near present-day Minneapolis. Zeb thought the site would be a good place to build a fort.

for two hundred dollars in trade goods. Fort Snelling was built on the site in 1820. Wilkinson later complained that Zeb paid too much for the land.

The party was a hundred miles farther north when winter struck. Determined to complete his mission, Zeb pressed on. The men built sleds and dragged them up the frozen river. Frostbite nipped at noses, toes, and fingers. Zeb ranged ahead, serving as hunter, guide, and scout. On December 23, the men covered a bare four miles. "Never did I undergo more fatigue," Zeb wrote.

On January 30, the weary group reached a fork in the river. Zeb took the western fork toward Leech Lake. The eastern fork led to Lake Itasca. Later surveys showed that Lake Itasca was the true source of the Mississippi.

Zeb met fur trader Hugh McGillis at Leech Lake. McGillis was a Scotsman who worked for a British company. A glance at the well-armed Americans convinced him that Zeb meant business. He listened to Zeb's speech about obeying U.S. laws. When Zeb finished, McGillis promised not to fly the British flag. He also agreed to pay the "common duties established by law." Despite his pledge, McGillis went back to his old ways after Zeb left.

His mission complete, Zeb turned south toward St. Louis. Heavy snows forced him to make part of the trip on snowshoes. When the ice broke up, Zeb and his men made canoes for the trip downriver. They reached St. Louis on April 30. In nine months, the expedition had explored five thousand miles of wilderness.

Chapter 5

Sand Like the Ocean's Rolling Wave

Zeb did not return to a hero's welcome. Only Clara and his family gave him a warm greeting. In a report to Congress, President Jefferson passed over the explorer's exploits in a single line. Zeb hurried to write his own report. "The preparations for my new voyage prevented the . . . correction of my errors," he said.

Just days after his return, Zeb's hopes for a long rest had vanished. General Wilkinson ordered him to mount an expedition to the Rocky Mountains. Soon, two keelboats were filling up with gunpowder, flour, and other supplies. Zeb packed a telescope and a supply of coffee. Because he thought the heat would be intense, he ordered cotton uniforms. Zeb and his men paid dearly for his mistake that winter.

THE EXPLORATIONS OF
ZEBULON PIKE
1805–1807

CANADA

MONTANA
NO. DAKOTA
Leech Lake
WYOMING
SO. DAKOTA
MINN
WISC
MICH
NY
York
L. Ontario
Site of future
Ft. Snelling
Battle of
Fallen Timbers
Lake Erie
PA
NEBRASKA
IOWA
OHIO
COLORADO
Pawnee Villages
ILLINOIS
INDIANA
Pikes Peak
MISSOURI
Ft. Washington
Ft. Knox
KANSAS
Osage
Villages
St. Louis
Ft. Kaskaskia
KENTUCKY
Pike picked up
by the Spanish
OKLA
ARK
Santa Fe
NEW
MEXICO
TEXAS
Natchitoches
LA
New Orleans
San Antonio
Chihuahua
MEXICO

············· Expedition of 1805–06
– – – – – – Expedition of 1806–07
All boundaries are shown as
they appear on today's maps.

Zebulon Pike made two epic journeys of exploration between 1805 and 1807. His first expedition took him to the headwaters of the Mississippi River. A few months later, he set out to explore the American Southwest. Zeb's reports later helped inspire the nation's westward movement.

Wilkinson's final orders came through on June 24, 1806. Zeb's first task was to return fifty-one Osage to their homes. The Osage had been held captive by an eastern tribe. Then, as he moved west, Zeb would hold peace talks with the plains tribes. Along the way, he would survey the Red and Arkansas rivers.

It seems clear that Wilkinson talked to Zeb about a spy mission. He said he needed to know more about Spain's defenses. Acting as a spy made sense to Zeb. If war broke out, the army would need firsthand information. Zeb most likely did not know his mentor's true plans. Wilkinson and Aaron Burr hoped to invade Mexico by following the trail Zeb would blaze.

Zeb added a doctor and an interpreter to his twenty-man team. The doctor was Wilkinson's friend, John Robinson, who also marched under orders to spy on the Spanish. Most of the soldiers were veterans of Zeb's northern trip. They joined only because he ordered them to do so. Lieutenant James Wilkinson, the general's son, also signed on.

The keelboats started up the Missouri River on July 15. Strong winds and heavy rains held progress to less than twenty miles a day. The proud Osage walked along the bank. Hunters ranged further afield, looking for game. To improve morale, Zeb sometimes held shooting matches. The riflemen fired flintlocks at small targets forty paces away. Zeb, a skilled marksman, often won his own contests.

In mid-August, the expedition found the Grand Osage Village in what is now eastern Kansas. Zeb had assumed that American Indians were unfeeling savages. He was surprised to see the former captives welcomed with cries of joy. Later, Zeb spoke to an Osage tribal council. He told the chiefs that President Jefferson wanted all tribes to live in peace. Then he gave them medals stamped with the Great Father's image.

At this point, the Osage River was too shallow for the keelboats. Zeb swapped the boats for supplies. His hosts nearly rebelled when he asked for horses. After hard bargaining, the Osage sold

At a tribal council, Zebulon Pike presented some Osage chiefs with Jefferson Peace Medals. He told them that the Great Father hoped that all tribes could live together peacefully.

Zeb some of their worst mounts. Within a week, most of the horses had broken down.

Zeb and his men moved steadily westward. They were among the first white Americans to cross the rolling prairie. "I saw in my route," he wrote in his journal, "tracts . . . where the wind had thrown up the sand in all the fanciful form of the ocean's rolling wave." He added that "not a speck of vegetable matter existed" on these plains. This report helped give rise to a long-lived myth. For many years, the western plains were known as the Great American Desert.

The expedition reached a large Pawnee village on September 25. Zeb learned that he had narrowly missed three hundred Spanish soldiers. He could see the path their horses had trampled through the tall grass. The soldiers had been searching for him.

The Pawnee had been ordered to stop Zeb's advance. Instead, Chief White Wolf welcomed his new guests. Zeb preached his words of peace, but the Pawnee ignored him. They were not ready to give up their warlike ways.

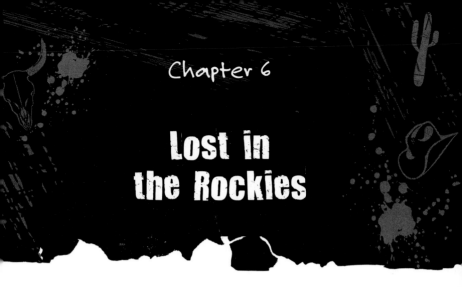

Chapter 6

Lost in the Rockies

On October 7, 1806, Zeb and his men were heading across Kansas. They rode with flintlocks primed. Bands of Pawnee followed, waving their guns and bows. Perhaps the soldiers looked too well armed. The warriors dropped back without firing a shot.

Zeb tried to follow a trail left by the Spanish. He soon lost it. Herds of buffalo and elk had erased any tracks. In years to come, this route would be called the Santa Fe Trail. In 1806, it was simply a trackless plain.

The Arkansas River came into view eight days later. The men started work on a buffalo-skin canoe and a dugout canoe. Zeb spent a pleasant hour watching a colony of prairie dogs. When the canoes were finished he split the party. As planned, young Wilkinson led a small group back down the Arkansas.

He thought his voyage to the Mississippi would take two to three weeks. Instead, it lasted seventy-three grueling days.

Zeb pushed west. He still hoped to find the source of the Arkansas River. The men feasted on buffalo, deer, and elk. They tried in vain to rope wild horses. On November 11, they crossed into what is now Colorado. A brisk north wind knifed through the men's lightweight uniforms. Zeb recalled the harsh weather of his last trip. "I determined to . . . accomplish every object even should it oblige me to spend another winter, in the desert," he wrote.

Game grew scarce. The horses tired, and two broke down. On November 15, Zeb caught his first glimpse of the Rockies. Ten days later he tried—and failed—to climb the peak that now bears his name. Back at his tiny fort, the dried buffalo meat was running low. If Zeb was worried, he did not let it show. He did give up on finding the source of the Arkansas. Dozens of streams flowed into the river. Any of them could have been the source.

When Zeb found a well-traveled trail, he followed it to the north. He was certain it would turn south to Santa Fe. Days later, he realized his mistake. Unsure of what to do, he turned back and struck the South

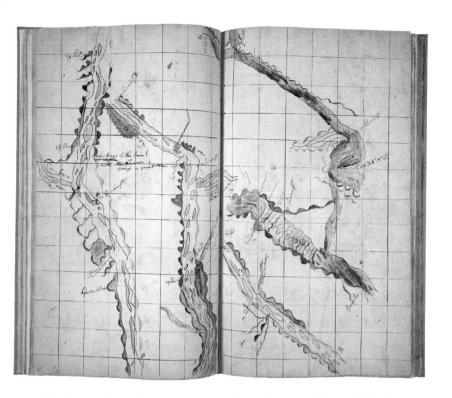

While searching for the source of the Arkansas River, Zebulon Pike and his party lost their way in the Rocky Mountains. While the men struggled through difficult terrain and harsh conditions, Zeb somehow found time to chart their progress. He drew this map in one of his notebooks during the 1806–1807 expedition.

Platte River. Leaving it after a few days, he stumbled on what he thought was the Red River. In fact, he was back on the Arkansas. The trailblazer was lost.

Winter struck with stunning force. Zeb's men cut up blankets to make socks and cloaks. Some limped along on frostbitten feet. At night, they slept on the ground near huge fires. Zeb described their misery: "[They lay] down at night on the snow or wet ground;

one side burning whilst the other was pierced with the cold wind." Christmas dinner was dried buffalo meat, eaten without salt.

Long stretches of the river were frozen. Zeb and his men built crude sleds to haul their supplies over the ice. In the Royal Gorge, the river plunged through a deep ravine. The men bypassed the rapids by climbing the cliffs above the gorge. As the valley widened, Zeb saw open prairie to the east. The date was January 5, 1807, his twenty-eighth birthday. He wrote: "Most fervently did I hope never to pass another [birthday] so miserably." By then he knew he had circled back to an old campsite.

A soldier shot six deer, ending the threat of starvation. Even so, Zeb knew his party was in poor shape. He told the men to build a small fort. Then he split his party. Two men stayed behind to guard the horses and baggage. Zeb, Dr. Robinson, and twelve soldiers set out to cross the mountains on foot. When they reached the Red River, they would send back for the others.

The men hobbled out of camp with seventy-pound packs on their backs. Zeb was one of the few who had not suffered frostbite. Despite the hardships, he had no intention of giving up. His spy mission drove him on.

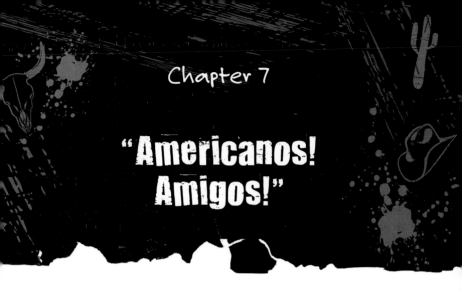

Chapter 7

"Americanos! Amigos!"

Zeb and his group forged on, mile after frozen mile. Nine of the men hobbled on frozen feet. By January 17, the food was gone. Zeb and Robinson went hunting. They wounded a buffalo, but the animal escaped. After a sleepless night, they took up the hunt again. At last, with hope and strength almost gone, Zeb brought down a buffalo. Weak from hunger, he drank some of the animal's blood.

Grilled steaks filled bellies but did not mend frozen feet. Two of the men could no longer walk. Zeb left them with some meat and promised to return. On January 22, he led the way south. When a hunting party killed three buffalo, Zeb freeze-dried the meat. The men took what they could carry and tied the rest to a raised platform. One of the injured men stayed behind to guard the cache.

During the day's march, Private John Brown lashed out. He complained about his heavy pack, the cold, and the poor food. That night, Zeb accused Brown of trying to start a mutiny. Repeat the offense, he warned, and pay with your life. Then he turned to the others. In a softer tone, he promised that their sacrifices would be rewarded.

Two days later, Zeb found a stream that ran west, not east. From the top of a sand hill he saw a large river through his spyglass. The river appeared to flow to the southeast. He told his men they were close to the Red River. The ragged column reached the waterway on January 30. There was no way for Zeb to know it was the Rio Grande.

For the first time in weeks, the men worried about American Indians. If they were attacked, they would need a fort. Zeb followed a westward-flowing stream until he found a wooded site. Looking back at the prairie below, he was moved by its beauty. Wildflowers were in bloom. Deer grazed on the islands that dotted the river. The snow-covered Sangre de Cristo mountains framed the scene. "It was . . . one of the most . . . beautiful inland prospects ever presented to the eyes of man," he wrote.

Zebulon Pike and his party built a stockade at a wooded site near the Rio Grande. Even as he rested his weary men, the explorer was making plans to continue his spy mission. In this 1820 illustration, a pack train crosses the desert on its way to the Spanish town of Santa Fe in present-day New Mexico.

The men cut trees and built a stockade of sharpened stakes. Walls enclosed a square thirty-six feet on each side. A plank led across a water-filled moat. With the fort finished, Zeb sent a party to bring in the men left behind. While he waited for them to return, he spent the time hunting and reading.

On February 7, Dr. Robinson set off alone for Santa Fe. Neither he nor Zeb had lost sight of their secret mission. The next eight days passed quietly, and the men strengthened the fort, hunted, and rested. The relief party returned with sad news. Two of the men were stranded, their toes lost to frostbite. In a message, the soldiers begged Zeb not to desert them. Zeb was distressed that they thought he might leave them behind. He quickly worked out a rescue plan.

On February 16, two riders approached the fort. Zeb greeted them with his limited Spanish. *"Americanos! Amigos,"* he called. Luckily, one of the men spoke French. He told Zeb that Robinson had reached Santa Fe. Zeb had his story ready. He said that his party was heading downriver to Natchitoches in Louisiana.

A hundred Spanish soldiers showed up ten days later. Lieutenant Fernandez brought a message from Governor Joaquin Alencaster. The governor had spoken to Robinson. He said he would be pleased to help the Americans reach the Red River. Zeb pretended to be shocked by the news that he was on Spanish soil. "What, said I, is not this the Red River?"

The Spanish were not fooled. Their own agents had warned that Wilkinson was sending a spy into their territory. Still playing Zeb's game, Fernandez invited him to meet the governor. Zeb left a few soldiers at the fort. They would wait for the men coming in from the mountains. Then he mounted a Spanish horse and set out for Santa Fe.

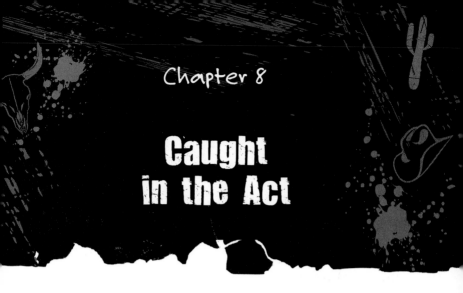

Chapter 8

Caught in the Act

In Santa Fe, curious eyes studied Zeb and his men. Zeb wore tattered blue pants and a coat made from a blanket. His scarlet cap was lined with fox skins. Most of his men had long beards and matted hair. He knew they looked like wild men. Someone in the crowd asked if Americans lived in houses.

Zeb was taken to the Palace of the Governors. He spoke to Governor Alencaster in French. His trespass, he said, was an honest mistake. Alencaster asked if Robinson had been part of Zeb's party. Fearful that the truth would brand Robinson as a spy, Zeb lied. He did not know that Alencaster already knew the truth.

The two men met again that night. Alencaster greeted Zeb and asked to see his papers. After Zeb read his orders aloud, the governor shook his hand. He said he was happy to meet a man of honor. Zeb thought

In this Frederic Remington print, Spanish soldiers escort Zebulon Pike and his men into Santa Fe. When the American party arrived in 1807, the Spanish gawked at the group's wild and unkempt appearance after months in the rugged wilderness.

that the danger was past, but Alencaster was no fool. A Spanish officer seized Zeb's papers the next day. Reading them convinced Alencaster that his guest *was* a spy.

Alencaster could have sentenced Zeb and his men to be shot. Instead, he sent the Americans south to Chihuahua for questioning. When he heard the order, Zeb asked if he and his party were prisoners. The governor said no but warned Zeb not to take any notes. His duty done, Alencaster treated Zeb to a fine dinner. Then he gave his guest one of his own shirts.

A troop of cavalry took the Americans south. The trail they followed was the *Camino Real* (Royal Highway). Zeb and his men were the first U.S. Army soldiers to set foot on the famous road. In Albuquerque, Father Ambrosia Guerra asked Zeb to supper. Zeb was quick to praise the young women who waited on him.

Dr. Robinson was waiting when Zeb reached his quarters. The doctor told Zeb of his talks with Alencaster. Now Zeb knew that the governor had seen through his lies. Still, the Spanish guards were quite lax. Zeb was free to write down what he saw and heard. His men hid the notes in their rifle barrels.

Lieutenant Don Facundo Melgares took charge of the escort on March 8. It was Melgares who had missed Zeb months before at the Pawnee camp. That night, Melgares put on a *fandango* in Zeb's honor. Young women flocked in from nearby villages to dance for the Americans. From that day on, the journey became one long party. On one day's march, two mules fell in the river. Zeb moaned that they had lost "an elegant assortment of biscuits."

The column reached Chihuahua on April 2. Governor Salcedo met Zeb and asked for a report of his trip. Zeb stuck to his story. Salcedo arranged for housing and settled down to read the explorer's papers.

Lieutenant Melgares and the Spanish townsfolk treated the Americans to a fandango in Zebulon Pike's honor. The festive dance, pictured here, was a welcome relief for Zeb and his crew after their long and dangerous journey.

What he read convinced him that Zeb and Robinson were spies. Still, he lacked hard proof. He could arrest the Americanos, but that might start a war. Salcedo decided to play it safe. He contented himself with sending a protest to the U.S. government.

In due course, Secretary of State James Madison replied to the note. He told the Spanish that "this government never employed a spy for any purpose." The Spanish, however, did not believe him. Government officials turned their anger on Salcedo and Alencaster.

Sending Zeb to Chihuahua, they said, allowed him to observe the region's defenses.

Zeb moved freely about the city. Noble Spanish families opened their doors to him. He had to borrow a thousand dollars from Salcedo to put on dinners of his own. On April 27, the governor said good-bye. A day later, the Americans started for home.

The return trip led east across Texas and into Louisiana. On July 1, Zeb rode into the frontier town of Natchitoches. He had been gone almost a year. The sight of his nation's flag filled his heart with pride. My country, he wrote, embraces "every tie which is dear to the soul of man!"

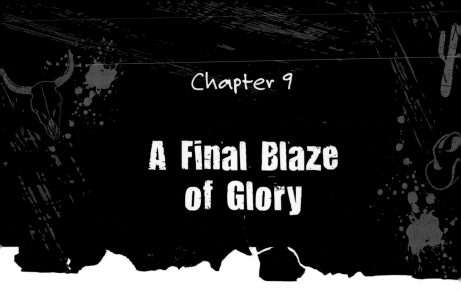

Chapter 9

A Final Blaze of Glory

Zeb returned to Washington with high hopes. His promotion to captain had come through. The press had given him a hero's welcome. Soon, however, the spotlight shifted to Aaron Burr's trial for treason. During the trial, General Wilkinson's involvement in Burr's plot came to light. Zeb's fame faded as his mentor's disgrace mounted.

Zeb's pleas for a high-level command fell on deaf ears. Wilkinson's enemies in Congress stood in his way. Undaunted, Zeb tried to win President Jefferson's backing by giving him a pair of grizzly cubs. He had carried the cubs back from his western journies in a cage. Jefferson was pleased—but he would not speak out on Zeb's behalf. The army sent Zeb back to his old post near St. Louis. A promotion to major helped ease his frustration.

In 1809, the United States and Britain were arguing over shipping rights. Zeb was assigned to General Wilkinson's staff at New Orleans. The new post pleased him. If war came, there was certain to be action around the busy port. Wilkinson chased business deals while his soldiers sweltered in the swamps. Zeb could do little to improve their lot. More than seven hundred soldiers died of malaria.

Wilkinson's superiors pressured him to take action. He responded by moving his headquarters northward. Zeb was left in charge. The command brought with it the rank of lieutenant colonel. It also upset officers who wanted the promotion for themselves. Without Wilkinson on hand to protect him, Zeb soon lost his post. For the next few years, the army moved him all over the South. His one chance at action came in western Louisiana. Bands of outlaws were living along the Sabine River. Zeb led the troops who swooped in and burned their camps.

War with Great Britain broke out in June 1812. The rush to expand the army brought Zeb a promotion to colonel. He raised a force of seven hundred New Yorkers and led them north. On November 21, the unit crossed into Canada near Plattsburg, New York. In a brief firefight, his men routed the British defenders.

This scene shows the death of Zebulon Pike during the American attack on York on April 27, 1813.

The gains were lost when Zeb's commander called off the invasion.

During the winter, Zeb drilled discipline and zeal into his men. In the spring, newly promoted to brigadier general, he moved to Lake Ontario. Across the lake, the British held the fortified town of York (now Toronto). On April 27, 1813, four thousand Americans stormed ashore from small boats. The defenders fled into the woods as Zeb's men advanced. The British commander saw that his men were beaten. He raised a white flag.

At that moment, a British powder storehouse blew up. The blast sent deadly chunks of stone flying through the air. A fragment struck Zeb in the back. Blood gushed from the wound as he fell. As his men gathered near, Zeb called out, "Push on, my brave fellows." A few hours later, he was dead.

Death brought Zebulon Pike the glory that life had denied him. President James Madison paid him a special tribute. The navy named a warship the *General Pike*. After the war, Zeb's journals kept his memory alive. Western settlers named rivers, lakes, and towns in his honor. Pikes Peak became a well-known landmark. In time, Zeb's mistakes were forgotten. His trailblazing exploits, however, are still remembered.

Pikes Peak, the mountaintop that immortalized Zebulon Pike's name, soars more than fourteen thousand feet into the Colorado skies. Every year, thousands of tourists, hikers, and climbers visit this National Historic Landmark.

Zeb had summed up his life in a last letter to his wife. "My dear Clara, . . . we shall attack at daylight," he wrote. "I shall dedicate these last moments to you, my love, and tomorrow throw all other ideas but my country to the wind."

What more can a nation ask of its heroes?

Glossary

cache—A hiding place.

Camino Real—Spanish for "Royal Highway," the road that led from Mexico City to the northern provinces.

cavalry—In the 1800s, an army unit trained to fight from horseback.

commission—A government document that appoints a candidate to a particular rank or office.

customs duties—Taxes that a country collects on goods imported from another country.

dispatches—Official messages that the sender wants delivered as quickly as possible.

duel—An armed combat between two people, usually fought under strict rules.

fandango—A type of Spanish dance and the music for it.

flintlock—An early firearm in which pulling the trigger causes a flint to produce a spark. The spark lights a powder charge that explodes and fires the weapon.

frostbite—Injury to the skin and underlying tissue caused by exposure to freezing temperatures.

Great Father—Zeb Pike used this name to refer to the president when negotiating with American Indians.

interpreter—Someone who translates one language into a second language.

journal—A written record of events in a person's life, often kept on a daily basis.

keelboat—A riverboat built for carrying freight.

latitude—The distance north or south of the earth's equator, measured in degrees along an imaginary line running from the North Pole to the South Pole.

Louisiana Purchase—The 1803 purchase from France of the vast region that lay between the Mississippi River and the Rocky Mountains.

malaria—A disease transmitted by the bite of a female *anopheles* mosquito.

militia—Part-time soldiers who are called to duty in times of emergency.

mutiny—Open rebellion by members of the armed forces against their commander.

Old Northwest—The name given in the early 1800s to the unsettled northwestern territories that later became the states of Illinois, Indiana, Ohio, Michigan, and Wisconsin.

quartermaster—The officer in charge of supplying food, clothing, and equipment to a military unit.

spyglass—A small telescope.

stockade—An enclosed area walled with sharpened stakes.

Further Reading

Books

Calvert, Patricia. *Zebulon Pike: Lost in the Rockies.* New York: Benchmark Books, 2005.

Doak, Robin S. *Zebulon Pike: Explorer and Soldier.* Minneapolis, Minn.: Compass Point Books, 2006.

Jones, Charlotte Foltz. *Westward Ho!: Eleven Explorers of the West.* New York: Holiday House, 2005.

Magoon, Kekla. *The Zebulon Pike Expedition.* Edina, Minn.: ABDO Publishing Company, 2009.

Witteman, Barbara. *Zebulon Pike: Soldier and Explorer.* Mankato, Minn.: Capstone Press, 2006.

Internet Addresses

City of Colorado Springs: Pikes Peak History
<http://www.springsgov.com/Page.aspx?NavID=86>

Pike National Trail Association: Zebulon Pike
<http://zebulonpike.org/index.html>

Zebulon Pike's Expedition to the Southwest 1806–1807
<http://www.santafetrailresearch.com/pike/expedition.html>

Index